7/26/8?

To Bill

Oh to be as wise as
Mr. Franklin. Happy
Birthday Love,

Gwee

SELECTIONS
FROM
POOR
RICHARD'S
ALMANACKS

SELECTIONS
FROM
POOR
RICHARD'S
ALMANACKS

BY BENJAMIN FRANKLIN

AVENEL BOOKS · NEW YORK

Copyright © 1982 by Crown Publishers, Inc.
All rights reserved.

This 1982 edition is published by Avenel Books,
distributed by Crown Publishers, Inc.

Manufactured in the United States of America

h g f e d c b a

Library of Congress Cataloging in Publication Data

Frankin, Benjamin, 1706–1790.
Selections from Poor Richard's almanacks.

1. Maxims, American.   I. Oehl, George.   II. Title.
PS749.A3   1981   818'.102   81-20550
ISBN: 0-517-362392

CONTENTS

FOREWORD

Already a successful printer and publisher of the *Philadelphia Gazette,* Franklin published the first of the *Poor Richard's Almanacks* in 1732. The name of the imaginary astrologer, Richard Saunders, was probably taken from an actual English almanac-maker of the seventeenth century, while the idea for the title came from his brother James, publisher of *Poor Robin's Almanack* in Newport. *Poor Richard's* was an instant success, going into three printings its first year. The number of printed editions increased until an unprecented 10,000 copies were selling annually throughout Philadelphia, as well as Newport, New York, Charleston, and Boston.

Almanacs in eighteenth-century America were extremely popular, often the only printed matter a colonial household contained—they held something of interest for everyone. In the words of Franklin biographer Carl Van Doren, "Almanacs, pocket size and paper-bound, calculated the tides and the changes of the moon, and claimed to forecast the weather. Almanacs were calendars. They furnished astrology for those who believed it. There were sometimes recipes in almanacs, and jokes and poems and maxims, and odd facts of many sorts. The skimpy margins of the calendar pages were a diary. Children might learn to read from almanacs." A successful almanac could be highly profitable, as well as providing a considerable boost to the reputation of its creator. Franklin apparently knew his readers.

Considering the circumstance of the typical eighteenth-century colonist, the character of Richard Saunders was one easily identified with. His style was colloquial; he would complain about his poverty, jealousy of rival philomaths, and the unequal profits collected by his printer. He maintained a good-natured argument with his wife Bridget, a strong-willed, conscientious individual of indisputably pioneer stock. Lives tedious and boring, and intellects stagnant for want of new thought, found welcome respite in the pages of *Poor Richard*. One could empathize with him, and learn from him at the same time.

Although the ideas contained in the *Poor Richard* aphorisms did not originate with Franklin—he relied on a number of sources, particularly two anthologies of verse, James Howell's *Lexicon Tetraglotton* (1660) and Thomas Fuller's *Gnomologia* (1732)—he did improve upon them. For example, the Scottish proverb "Fat housekeepers make lean executors" he simplified to "A fat kitchen, a lean will," and he changed "A gloved cat was never a good hunter" to "The cat in gloves catches no mice." Discriminatingly selected, they reflected Franklin's philosophy on life, advocating prudence, order in human life, morality, industry, frugality, and humanity. Franklin the diplomat warns,

"There is no little enemy" and "Be slow in choosing a Friend, slower in changing"; Franklin the successful businessman instructs, "Drive thy business or it will drive thee" and "The borrower is a Slave to the Lender; the Security to both." As Carl Van Doren noted, Richard Saunders provided Franklin with "a dramatic licence to speak as he chose. He could pretend to be an astrologer and yet make fun of superstition. He could pretend to be old and wise, packing his almanac with wisdom in the verses and proverbs which were all he had space for."

After 250 years, the aphorisms from *Poor Richard's Almanacks* are still quite popular, and are heard reiterated in conversation. This book is an attempt at illuminating their timelessness. It is, admittedly, subjective. Benjamin Franklin—tradesman, civil servant, diplomat, statesman, scientist, inventor, author, philosopher, founding father—epitomized the Renaissance man of his age. I hope that *Selections from Poor Richard's Almanacks* will provide a greater insight into the character of this fascinating individual, as well as proving relevant to our times.

GEORGE OEHL

Beware of him that is slow to anger: He is angry for something, and will not be pleased for nothing.

ANGER
&
PASSION

Are you angry that others disappoint you?
remember you cannot depend upon yourself.

> *Anger* is never without a Reason,
> but seldom with a good One.

Anger warms the Invention, but overheats the Oven.

> Take heed of the Vinegar of sweet Wine,
> and the Anger of Good-nature.

Take this remark from *Richard* poor and lame,
Whate'er's begun in anger ends in shame.

Beware of him that is slow to anger: He is angry
for some thing, and will not be pleased for nothing.

The too obliging Temper is evermore disobliging itself.

A Temper to bear much, will have much to bear.

He that cannot bear with other People's Passions, cannot govern his own.

The end of Passion is the beginning of Repentance.

If *Passion* drives, Let *Reason* hold the Reins.

A Man in a Passion rides a mad Horse.

Nick's Passions grow fat and hearty; his Understanding looks consumptive!

VANITY, MODESTY, & HUMILITY

Humility makes great men twice honourable.

He that falls in love with himself, will have no Rivals.

Prythee isn't Miss *Cloe's* a comical Case?
She lends out her Tail, and she borrows her Face.

If thou hast wit & learning, add to it Wisdom and Modesty.

A Flatterer never seems absurd:
The Flatter'd always take his Word.

Poverty, Poetry, and new Titles of Honour, make Men ridiculous.

Great Modesty often hides great Merit.

Happy *Tom Crump,* ne'er sees his own Hump.

Wide will wear, but Narrow will tear.

Vanity backbites more than *Malice.*

There have been as great Souls unknown to fame as any of the most famous.

What is a butterfly? At best
He's but a caterpiller drest,
The gaudy Fop's his picture just.

To all apparent Beauties blind
Each Blemish strikes an envious Mind.

Why does the blind man's wife paint herself?

She that paints her Face, thinks of her Tail.

Vain-Glory flowereth, but beareth no Fruit.

Honours change Manners.

Tom, vain's your Pains; They all will fail:
Ne'er was good Arrow made of a Sow's Tail.

Nothing humbler than *Ambition,* when it is about to climb.

When out of Favour, none know thee;
when in, thou dost not know thyself.

Beauty & folly are old companions.

He that is conscious of a Stink in his Breeches,
is jealous of every Wrinkle in another's Nose.

Bess brags she 'as *Beauty,* and can prove the same:
As how? why thus, Sir, 'tis her *puppy's* name.

A quiet Conscience sleeps in Thunder,
but Rest and Guilt live far asunder.

CONSCIENCE

E're you remark another's Sin,
Bid your own Conscience look within.

There are three Things extreamly hard, Steel,
a Diamond and to know one's self.

The nearest way to come at glory,
is to do that for conscience which we do for glory.

Keep Conscience clear,
Then never fear.

A quiet Conscience sleeps in Thunder,
but Rest and Guilt live far asunder.

Would you live with ease,
Do what you ought, and not what you please.

He that doth what he should not,
shall feel what he would not.

What you would seem to be, be really.

If thou injurest Conscience, it will have its Revenge on thee.

Some make Conscience of wearing a Hat in the Church, who make none of robbing the Altar.

HEALTH

Early to bed and early to rise, makes a man healthy wealthy and wise.

Sal laughs at every thing you say. Why? Because she has fine Teeth.

Be not sick too late, nor well too soon.

Keep your mouth wet, feet dry.

Maids of *America,* who gave you bad teeth? *Answ.* Hot Soupings & frozen Apples.

Hot things, sharp things, sweet things, cold things All rot the teeth, and make them look like old things.

Laws *too gentle* are seldom *obeyed;*
too severe, seldom *executed.*

JUSTICE
&
THE LAW

I'll go to Law. Right, said his Friend, for if you go to
law, I am sure you don't consider.

What pains our Justice takes his faults to hide,
With half that pains sure he might cure 'em quite.

Nothing brings more pain than too much pleasure;
nothing more bondage than too much liberty, (or
libertinism).

Sudden Power is apt to be insolent, *Sudden Liberty*
saucy; that behaves best which has grown gradually.

Without justice, courage is weak.

The magistrate should obey the Laws,
the People should obey the magistrate.

Where there is Hunger, Law is not regarded; and
where Law is not regarded, there will be Hunger.

Laws *too gentle* are seldom *obeyed;*
too severe, seldom *executed.*

Where there's no Law, there's no Bread.

Where carcasses are, eagles will gather,
And where good laws are, much people flock thither.

GOD
&
RELIGION

In the Affairs of this World Men are saved, not by Faith, but by the Want of it.

Talking against Religion is unchaining a Tyger;
The Beast let loose may worry his Deliverer.

The Heathens when they dy'd, went to Bed without a Candle.

Take Courage, Mortal; Death can't banish thee out of the Universe.

Don't judge of Mens Wealth or Piety,
by their *Sunday* Appearances.

Danger is Sauce for Prayers.

How many observe Christ's Birth-day! How few, his Precepts! O! 'tis easier to keep Holidays than Commandments.

If wind blows on you thro' a hole,
Make your will and take care of your soul.

The Bell calls others to Church,
but itself never minds the Sermon.

The painful Preacher, like a candle bright,
Consumes himself in giving others Light.

Nature and nature's laws lay hid in night;
God said, Let NEWTON be, *and all was light.*

Sin is not hurtful because it is forbidden
but it is forbidden because it's hurtful.

He that lives carnally, won't live eternally.

Some are justly laught at for keeping their Money foolishly, others for spending it idly: He is the greatest fool that lays it out in a purchase of repentance.

'Tis not a Holiday that's not kept holy.

Eyes and Priests
Bear no Jests.

Eyes and Priests
Bear no Jests.

Think of three Things, whence you came, where you are
going, and to whom you must account.

Sam's Religion is like a Chedder Cheese, 'tis made
of the milk of one & twenty Parishes.

He that resolves to mend hereafter,
resolves not to mend now.

That Ignorance makes devout, if right the Notion,
'Troth, Rufus, thou'rt a Man of great Devotion.

Anger and Folly walk cheek by-jole;
Repentance treads on both their Heels.

Does Mischief, Misconduct, & Warrings displease ye;
Think there's a Providence, 'twill make ye easy.

Serving God is Doing Good to Man, but Praying is
thought an easier Service, and therefore more generally
chosen.

Fear not death; for the sooner we die
the longer shall we be immortal.

Fear not Death; for the sooner we die
the longer shall we be immortal.

The Way to see by *Faith,* is to shut the Eye of *Reason:*
The Morning Daylight appears plainer when you put
out your Candle.

Prayers and Provender hinder no Journey.

When Knaves fall out, honest Men get their goods:
When Priests dispute, we come at the Truth.

If worldly Goods cannot save me from Death,
they ought not to hinder me of eternal Life.

Christianity commands us to pass by Injuries;
Policy, to let them pass by us.

Different Sects like different clocks,
may be all near the matter, 'tho they don't quite agree.

Work as if you were to live 100 years,
Pray as if you were to die To-morrow.

Many have quarrel'd about Religion, that never
practis'd it.

No Resolution of Repenting hereafter, can be sincere.

What is Serving God? 'Tis doing Good to Man.

Many a long dispute among Divines may be thus
abridg'd, It is so: It is not so, It is so; It is not so.

If God blesses a Man, his Bitch brings forth Pigs.

God, *Parents,* and *Instructors,* can never be requited.

Fear God, and your Enemies will fear you.

Keep thou from the Opportunity,
and God will keep thee from the Sin.

He that would have a short Lent,
Let him borrow Money to be repaid at Easter.

To err is human, to repent divine, to persist devilish.

When Death puts out our Flame, the Snuff will tell,
If we were Wax, or Tallow by the Smell.

He that carries a small Crime easily,
will carry it on when it comes to be an Ox.

HONESTY
&
DISHONESTY

Men take more pains to mask than mend.

Beware, beware! he'll cheat 'ithout scruple, who can without fear.

Tis hard (but glorious) to be poor and honest: An empty Sack can hardly stand upright; but if it does, 'tis a stout one!

An hundred Thieves cannot strip one naked Man, especially if his Skin's off.

He that carries a small Crime easily, will carry it on when it comes to be an Ox.

There is neither honour nor gain, got in dealing with a vil-lain.

Craft must be at charge for clothes,
but *Truth* can go naked.

It is wise not to seek a Secret, and Honest not to reveal it.

The honest Man takes Pains, and then enjoys Pleasures; the Knave takes Pleasure, and then suffers Pains.

Half the Truth is often a great Lie.

O Maltster! break that cheating Peck; 'tis plain,
When e'er you use it, you're a Knave in Grain.

Little Rogues easily become great Ones.

Ambition often spends foolishly what *Avarice* had wickedly collected.

Little Rogues easily become great Ones.

It's common for Men to give pretended Reasons instead of one real one.

Trust thy self, and another shall not betray thee.

Who has deceiv'd thee so oft as thy self?

It's the easiest Thing in the World for a Man to deceive himself.

Honest *Tom*! you may trust him with a house-full of untold Milstones.

When Knaves betray each other, one can scarce be blamed, or the other pitied.

A Lie stands on 1 leg, Truth on 2.

Every Man has Assurance enough to boast of his honesty, few of their Understanding.

An honest Man will receive neither *Money* nor *Praise,* that is not his Due.

Do not do that which you would not have known.

Rob not for burnt offerings.

You may talk too much on the best of subjects.

DISCRETION

The Tongue offends, and the Ears get the cuffing.

When Man and Woman die, as Poets sung,
His Heart's the last part moves, her last, the tongue.

Speak with contempt of none, from slave to king,
The meanest Bee hath, and will use, a sting.

There's small Revenge in Words, but Words
may be greatly revenged.

Mary's mouth costs her nothing,
for she never opens it but at others expence.

A soft Tongue may strike hard.

Teach your child to hold his tongue,
he'll learn fast enough to speak.

The Tongue is ever turning to the aching Tooth.

Man's tongue is soft, and bone doth lack;
Yet a stroke therewith may break a man's back.

Tongue double, brings trouble.

If you have no Honey in your Pot, have some in your
Mouth.

Harry Smatter, has a Mouth for every Matter.

You may talk too much on the best of subjects.

Let thy Discontents be Secrets.

None are deceived but they that confide.

Nor Eye in a letter, nor Hand in a purse,
nor Ear in the secret of another.

Three may keep a Secret, if two of them are dead.

> To whom thy secret thou dost tell,
> To him thy freedom thou dost sell,

A Slip of the Foot you may soon recover:
But a Slip of the Tongue you may never get over.

In a corrupt Age, the putting the World in order would
breed Confusion; then e'en mind your own Business.

Paintings and Fightings are best seen at a distance.

There's a time to wink as well as to see.

Courage would fight, but *Discretion* won't let him.

Hide not your Talents, they for Use were made.
What's a Sun-Dial in the Shade!

Let all Men know thee, but no man know thee
thoroughly: Men freely ford that see the shallows.

He that speaks much, is much mistaken.

Lovers, Travellers, and Poets, will give money to be heard.

Great talkers should be cropt, for they've no need of ears.

Here comes *Glib-tongue*: who can out-flatter a Dedication; and lie, like ten Epitaphs.

Speak and speed: the close mouth catches no flies.

Clearly spoken, Mr. Fog! You explain English by Greek.

Silence is not always a Sign of Wisdom, but Babbling is ever a Mark of Folly.

Many a Man's own Tongue gives Evidence against his Understanding.

None preaches better than the ant, and she says nothing.

A Pair of good Ears will drain dry an hundred Tongues.

If you would keep your Secret from an enemy, tell it not to a friend.

Let thy discontents be thy Secrets;—if the world knows them, 'twill despise *thee* and increase *them*.

The World is full of fools and faint hearts, and yet every one has courage enough to bear the misfortunes, and wisdom enough to manage the Affairs of his neighbour.

You may give a Man an Office,
but you cannot give him Discretion.

In a discreet man's mouth, a publick thing is private.

When you're an Anvil, hold you still;
When you're a Hammer, strike your Fill.

Proclaim not all thou knowest, all thou owest,
all thou hast, nor all thou canst.

Those who in quarrels interpose,
Must often wipe a bloody nose.

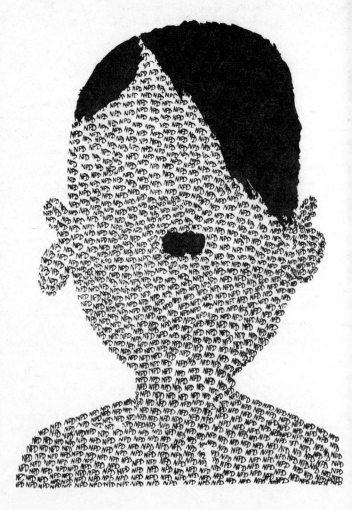

Ignorance leads men into the Party,
and *Shame* keeps them from getting out again.

KINGS,
PRINCES,
&
POLITICS

Children and Princes will quarrel for Trifles.

Friends are the true Sceptres of Princes.

Ignorance leads Men into a Party,
and *Shame* keeps them from getting out again.

On him true HAPPINESS shall wait
Who shunning noisy Pomp and State

In Rivers & bad Governments, the lightest Things
swim at top.

The greatest monarch on the proudest throne,
is oblig'd to sit upon his own arse.

Kings and Bears often worry their Keepers.

George came to the Crown without striking a Blow.
Ah! quoth the Pretender, would I could do so.

The King's cheese is half wasted in parings;
but no matter, 'tis made of the peoples milk.

Kings & Bears often worry their keepers.

The church the state, and the poor, are 3 daughters
which we should maintain, but not portion off.

Came you from Court? for in your Mien,
A self-important air is seen.

He that would rise at Court, must begin by Creeping.

An innocent *Plowman* is more worthy than a vicious
Prince.

The Good-will of the Governed will be starv'd,
if not fed by the good Deeds of the Governors.

Many Princes sin with *David,* but few repent with him.

Kings and Bears often worry their Keepers.

A little well-gotten will do us more good,
Than lordships and scepters by Rapine and Blood.

Kings have long Arms, but Misfortune longer:
Let none think themselves out of her Reach.

The royal Crown cures not the Head-ach.

CRITICISM

The Sting of a Reproach, is the Truth of it.

He that sows thorns, should not go barefoot.

He that would live in peace & at ease,
Must not speak all he knows, nor judge all he sees.

Don't throw stones at your neighbours,
if your own windows are glass.

Clean your Finger, before you point at my Spots.

Praise little, dispraise less.

He that can bear a Reproof, and mend by it,
if he is not wise, is in a fair way of being so.

He is not well-bred, that cannot bear Ill-Breeding in others.

Bad Commentators spoil the best of books
So God sends meat (they say) the devil Cooks.

He has lost his Boots but sav'd his spurs.

In other men we faults can spy,
And blame the mote that dims their eye;
Each little speck and blemish find;
To our own stronger errors blind.

Tell me my Faults, and mend your own.

The worst wheel of the cart makes the most noise.

Observe all men; thy self most.

Wink at small faults; remember thou has great ones.

Who says Jack is not generous? he is always fond of giving, and cares not for receiving.—What? Why; Advice.

FOOD
&
DRINK

Do me the Favour to deny me at once.

He that spills the Rum, loses that only; He that drinks it, often loses both that and himself.

Sleep without Supping, and you'll rise without owing for it.

He that never eats too much, will never be lazy.

No wonder *Tom* grows fat, th' unwieldy Sinner
Makes his whole Life but one continual Dinner.

Three good meals a day is bad living.

Too much plenty makes Mouth dainty.

When the Wine enters, out goes the Truth.

Eat to live, and not live to eat.

He that would travel much, should eat little.

Tim moderate fare and abstinence much prizes,
In publick, but in private gormandizes.

Take counsel in wine, but resolve afterwards in water.

Nice Eaters seldom meet with a good Dinner.

Hold your Council before Dinner;
the full Belly hates Thinking as well as Acting.

To avoid Pleurisies, &c. in cool Weather; Fevers, Fluxes,
&c. in hot; beware of *Over-Eating and Over-Heating*.

Drunkenness, that worst of Evils, makes some Men
Fools, some Beasts, some Devils.

Eat to live, and not live to eat.

A full Belly is the Mother of all Evil.

Drink does not drown *Care,* but waters it,
and makes it grow faster.

Be temperate in wine, in eating, girls, & sloth;
Or the Gout will seize you and plague you both.

There's more old Drunkards than old Doctors.

Dine with little, sup with less:
Do better still; sleep supperless.

A fat kitchin, a lean Will.

Never spare the Parson's wine, nor Baker's Pudding.

A wolf eats sheep but now and then,
Ten Thousands are devour'd by Men.

If it were not for the Belly, the Back might wear Gold.

Never spare the Parson's wine, nor the Baker's pudding.

Nothing more like a Fool, than a drunken man.

Finikin *Dick,* curs'd with nice Taste,
Ne'er meets with good dinner, half starv'd at a feast.

To lengthen thy Life, lessen thy Meals.

A full Belly brings forth every Evil.

After feasts made, the maker scratches his head.

Eat few Suppers, and you'll need few Medicines.

Poor Dick, eats like a well man, and drinks like a sick.

A full Belly makes a dull Brain: The Muses
starve in a Cook's Shop.

Cheese and salt meat, should be sparingly eat.

He that steals the old man's supper, do's him no wrong.

Nothing more like a Fool, than a drunken Man.

Never mind it, she'l be sober after the Holidays.

Rather go to bed supperless, than run in debt for a Breakfast.

He that drinks his Cyder alone,
let him catch his Horse alone.

Drink Water, Put the Money in your Pocket, and leave the *Dry-bellyach* in the *Punchbowl.*

Wealth is not his that has it, but his that enjoys it.

WEALTH, FRUGALITY, & MISERLINESS

If your Riches are yours, why don't you take them
with you to the t'other World?

Money and good Manners make the Gentleman.

Wealth is not his that has it, but his that enjoys it.

There are three faithful friends,
an old wife, an old dog, and ready money.

Wish a miser long life, and you wish him no good.

Necessity has no Law; Why? Because
'tis not to be had without Money.

Nothing but Money,
Is sweeter than Honey.

Tell a miser he's rich, and a woman she's old,
you'll get no money of one, nor kindness of t'other.

Avarice and Happiness never saw each other,
how then shou'd they become acquainted.

The miser's cheese is wholesomest.

But at his Heart, the most undaunted Son
Of Fortune, dreads its Name and awful Charms.

He does not possess Wealth, it possesses him.

There is much money given to be laught at,
though the purchasers don't know it;
witness *A's* fine horse, & *B's* fine house.

A large train makes a light Purse.

Silks and Sattins put out the Kitchen Fire.

Ask and have, is sometimes dear buying.

All things are cheap to the saving, dear to the wasteful.

Gifts much expected, are *paid,* not *given.*

If you know how to spend less than you get,
you have the Philosophers-Stone.

Spare and have is better than *spend and crave.*

'Tis a well spent penny that saves a groat.

If you'd have a Servant that you like, serve your self.

Many have been ruin'd by buying good pennyworths.

A light purse is a heavy Curse.

Poverty wants some things, Luxury many things,
Avarice all things.

He that can travel well afoot, keeps a good horse.

He that buys by the penny, maintains not only himself,
but other people.

Beware of little Expences,
a small Leak will sink a great Ship.

Buy what thou hast no need of;
and e'er long thou shalt sell thy necessaries.

The thrifty maxim of the wary *Dutch,*
Is to save all the Money they can touch.

Light purse, heavy heart.

At a great Pennyworth, pause a while.

Old Boys have their Playthings as well as young Ones;
the Difference is only in the Price.

Patience in Market, is worth Pounds in a Year.

Light Gains heavy Purses.

He that is rich need not live sparingly,
and he that can live sparingly need not be rich.

CONTENTMENT

Content makes poor men rich; Discontent makes rich Men poor.

None know the unfortunate, and the fortunate do not know themselves.

When you taste Honey, remember Gall.

Who is rich? He that rejoices in his Portion.

He that hath no *ill* Fortune will be troubled with *good*.

If you desire many things, many things will seem but a few.

Blessed is he that expects nothing,
for he shall never be disappointed.

Better is a little with content than much with
contention.

He that's content, hath enough;
He that complains, has too much.

He that builds before he counts the Cost, acts foolishly;
and he that counts before he builds, finds he did not
count wisely.

In success be moderate.

Money & Man a mutual Friendship show:
Man makes *false* Money, Money makes Man so.

Success has ruin'd many a Man.

When *Prosperity* was well mounted, she let go the
Bridle, and soon came tumbling out of the Saddle.

Dally not with other Folks Women or Money.

The poor have little, beggars none,
the rich too much, *enough* not one.

The Poor have little, Beggars none;
the Rich too much, enough not one.

If Man could have Half his Wishes,
he would double his Troubles.

Content and Riches seldom meet together,
Riches take thou, contentment I had rather.

We are not so sensible of the greatest Health
as of the least Sickness.

From Madmen's Hands I did my Wealth receive,
Therefore that Wealth to Madmen's Hands I leave.

The good Pay-master is Lord of another man's Purse.

Many a Man would have been worse,
if his Estate had been better.

The generous Mind least regards money,
and yet most feels the Want of it.

Empty Freebooters, cover'd with Scorn:
They went out for Wealth, & come ragged and torn,
As the Ram went for Wool, and was sent back shorn.

Wealth and Content are not always Bed-fellows.

He that is of Opinion Money will do every Thing,
man well be suspected of doing every Thing for Money.

A Man has no more *Goods* than he gets Good by.

A rich rogue, is like a fat hog, who never does good
til as dead as a log.

He who multiplies Riches multiplies Cares.

He that waits upon Fortune, is never sure of a Dinner.

Hunger never saw bad bread.

POVERTY

Great famine when wolves eat wolves

When the Well's dry, we know the Worth of Water.

For one poor Man there are an hundred indigent.

Pox take you, is no curse to some people.

Many a Meal is lost for want of meat.

Hunger never saw bad bread.

Having been poor is no shame, but being ashamed of it, is.

I saw few die of Hunger, of Eating 100000.

The poor man must walk to get meat for his stomach,
the rich man to get a stomach to his meat.

What one relishes, nourishes.

An empty Bag cannot stand upright.

LAWYERS
&
DOCTORS

Necessity has no Law; I know some Attorneys of the name.

> No workman without tools,
> No Lawyer without Fools,
> Can live by their Rules.

God heals, and the Doctor takes the Fees.

He's the best physician that knows the worthlessness of the most medicines.

> A good Lawyer a bad Neighbour.

> It is ill Jesting with the Joiner's Tools,
> worse with the Doctor's.

Don't go to the doctor with every distemper, nor to the lawyer with every quarrel, nor to the pot for every thirst.

A countryman between 2 Lawyers,
is like a fish between two cats.

Many dishes many diseases.
Many medicines few cures.

God works wonders now & then;
Behold! a Lawyer, an honest Man!

Beware of the young Doctor & the old Barber.

Don't misinform your Doctor nor your Lawyer.

He's a Fool that makes his Doctor his Heir.

Lawyers, Preachers, and Tomtits Eggs,
there are more of them hatch'd than come to perfection.

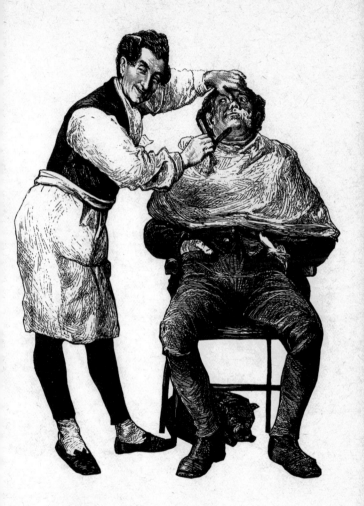

Beware of the young Doctor & the old Barber.

Ceremony is not Civility, nor Civility Ceremony.

CIVILITY

Eat to please thyself, but dress to please others.

Be not niggardly of what costs thee nothing,
as courtesy, counsel, & countenance.

Be civil to *all*; serviceable to *many*; familiar with few;
Friend to *one*; Enemy to *none*.

Ceremony is not Civility; nor Civility Ceremony.

Friendship increases by visiting Friends,
but by visiting seldom.

Visits should be short, like a winters day,
Lest you're too troublesom hasten away.

Visit your Aunt, but not every Day;
and call at your Brother's, but not every night.

After 3 days men grow weary, of a wench, a guest,
& weather rainy.

When you speak to a man, look on his eyes;
when he speaks to thee, look on his mouth.

Full of courtesie, full of craft.

Fish & Visitors stink in 3 days.

Ill Customs & bad Advice are seldom forgotten.

TIME

Haste Makes Waste.

The hasty Bitch brings forth blind Puppies.

If you'd have it done, Go: If not, send.

Necessity never made a good bargain.

Employ thy time well, if thou meanest to gain leisure.

One *To-day* is worth two *To-morrows*.

Prodigality of *Time,* produces Poverty of Mind as well as of Estate.

To-morrow, every Fault is to be amended;
but that *To-morrow* never comes.

Neglect mending a small Fault,
and 'twill soon be a great One.

If you have time don't wait for time.

Time *eateth* all things, could old Poets say;
The Times are chang'd, our times *drink* all away.

Make haste slowly.

An Egg to day is better than a Hen to-morrow.

Time is an herb that cures all Diseases.

Time enough, always proves *little enough.*

Dost thou love Life? then do not squander Time;
for that's the Stuff Life is made of.

You may delay, but *Time* will not.

Employ thy time well, if thou meanest to gain leisure.

Don't think to hunt two hares with one dog.

He that can take rest is greater than he that can take cities.

Have you somewhat to do to-morrow; do it to-day.

Idleness is the greatest Prodigality.

Since thou art not sure of a minute,
throw not away an hour.

Lost Time is never found again.

Many estates are spent in the getting,
Since women for tea forsook spinning & knitting.

He that riseth late, must trot all day,
and shall scarce overtake his business at night.

It is not Leisure that is not used.

Look before, or you'll find yourself behind.

PRIDE

Pride breakfasted with *Plenty,* dined with *Poverty,* supped with *Infamy.*

Pride is as loud a Beggar as *Want,* and a great deal more saucy.

As sore places meet most rubs, proud folks meet most affronts.

The D——l wipes his B——ch with poor Folks Pride.

Mark with what insolence and pride, Blown *Bufo* takes his haughty stride; As if no toad was toad beside.

Fond Pride of Dress is sure an empty Curse; E're *Fancy* you consult, consult your Purse.

Men meet, mountains never.

Great Pride and Meanness sure are near ally'd;
Or thin Partitions do their Bounds divide.

Pride gets into the Coach, and *Shame* mounts behind.

Pride and the *Gout,* are seldom cur'd throughout.

As Pride increases, Fortune declines.

Declaiming against Pride, is not always a Sign of
Humility.

To be *proud* of *Knowledge,* is to be *blind* with *Light;* to
be *proud* of *Virtue,* is to *poison* yourself with the
Antidote.

The Proud hate Pride—in others.

Great Merit is coy, as well as great Pride.

Pride dines upon Vanity, sups on Contempt.

BUSINESS

Neither trust, nor contend, nor lay wagers, nor lend;
And you'll have peace to your Lives end.

> He is no clown that drives the plow,
> but he that doth clownish things.

Get what you can, and what you get, hold;
'Tis the *Stone* that will turn all your Lead into Gold.

If you'd be wealthy, think of saving, more than of
getting: The *Indies* have not made *Spain* rich, because
her Outgoes equal her Incomes.

> *Sell-cheap* kept Shop on *Goodwin Sands*,
> and yet had Store of Custom.

Receive before you write, but write before you pay.

Bad Gains are truly Losses.

The first Mistake in publick Business, is the going into it.

When a Friend deals with a Friend
Let the Bargain be clear and well penn'd,
That they may continue Friends to the End.

Tim and his Handsaw are good in their Place,
Tho' not fit for preaching or shaving a face.

Idleness is the Dead Sea, that swallows all Virtues: Be
active in Business, that *Temptation* may miss her Aim:
The Bird that sits, is easily shot.

If you'd know the Value of Money, go and borrow some.

The Creditors are a superstitious sect,
great observers of set days and times.

Creditors have better memories than debtors.

'Tis against some Mens Principle to pay Interest,
and seems against others Interest to pay the Principal.

Drive thy Business, or it will drive thee.

He's gone, and forgot nothing but to say *Farewel*—
to his creditors.

The *Borrower* is a Slave to the *Lender*; the *Security* to
both.

Great spenders are bad lenders.

Pay what you owe, and you'll know what's your own.

Pay what you owe, and what you're worth you'll know.

Industry pays Debts, Despair encreases them.

If you'd lose a troublesome Visitor, lend him Money.

Lying rides upon Debt's back.

Drive thy Business, or it will drive thee.

He that has a Trade, has an Office of Profit and Honour.

Industry, Perseverance, & Frugality, make Fortune
yield.

Not to oversee Workmen, is to leave them your Purse open.

No gains without pains.

The way to be safe, is never to be secure.

He that hath a Trade, hath an Estate.

He that pays for Work before it's done, has but a pennyworth for twopence.

A Change of *Fortune* hurts a wise Man no more than a Change of the *Moon*.

Those that have much Business must have much Pardon.

Discontented Minds, and Fevers of the Body are not to be cured by changing Beds or Businesses.

Keep thy shop, & thy shop will keep thee.

Great Estates may venture more; Little Boats must keep near Shore.

Bargaining has neither friends nor relations.

He that sells upon trust, loses many friends, and always wants money.

Where bread is wanting, all's to be sold.

MARRIAGE

Marry your Daughter and eat fresh Fish betimes.

Old *Hob* was lately married in the Night,
What needed Day, his fair young Wife is light.

The proof of gold is fire, the proof of woman, gold;
the proof of man, a woman.

Wife from thy Spouse each blemish hide
More than from all the World beside:
Let *Decency* be all thy Pride.

He that goes far to marry,
will either deceive or be deceived.

Kate would have *Thomas,* no one blame her can:
Tom won't have *Kate,* and who can blame the Man?

As to his Wife, *John* minds St. *Paul,* He's one
That hath a Wife and is as if he'd none.

Forbear, quoth *Sam,* that fruitless Curse so common,
He'll not hurt me who've married his Kinswoman.

Punch-coal, cut-candle, and set brand on end,
is neither good house-wife, nor good house-wife's friend.

If *Jack's* in love, he's no judge of *Jill's* Beauty.

Three things are men most liable to be cheated in,
a Horse, a Wig, and a Wife.

A good Wife lost is God's gift lost.

Ne'er take a wife till thou hast a house (& a fire)
to put her in.

A good Wife & Health, is a Man's best Wealth.

Marry your Son when you will,
but your Daughter when you can.

Happy's the Wooing that's not long a doing.

Marry your Son when you will,
but you Daughter when you can.

A Man with out a Wife, is but half a Man.

The good or ill hap of a good or ill life,
is the good or ill choice of a good or ill wife.

He that has not got a Wife, is not yet a compleat Man.

Marry above thy match, and thou'lt get a Master.

I never saw an oft-transplanted tree,
Nor yet an oft-removed family,
That throve so well as those that settled be.

If you want a neat wife, chuse her on a Saturday.

A little House well fill'd, a little Field well till'd,
and a little Wife well will'd, are great Riches.

Where there's Marriage without Love,
there will be Love without Marriage.

Grief for a dead Wife, & a troublesome Guest,
Continues to the *threshold,* and there is at rest;
But I mean such wives as are none of the best.

Famine, Plague, War, and an unnumber'd throng
Of Guilt-avenging Ills, to Man belong;
Is't not enough Plagues, Wars, and Famines rise
To lash our crimes, but must our Wives be wise?

An undutiful Daughter, will prove an unmanageable
Wife.

Light heel'd mothers make leaden-heel'd daughters.

You can bear your own Faults,
and why not a Fault in your Wife.

A house without woman & Firelight, is like a body
without soul or sprite.

You cannot pluck roses without fear of thorns,
Nor enjoy a fair wife without danger of horns.

One good Husband is worth two good Wives; for the
scarcer things are the more they're valued.

He that takes a wife, takes care.

Good wives and good plantations are made by good husbands.

Jane, why those tears? why droops your head?
Is then your other husband dead?
Or doth a worse disgrace betide?
Hath no one since his death apply'd?

Keep your eyes wide open before marriage,
half shut afterwards.

FRIENDS
&
ENEMIES

Tart Words make no Friends: a spoonful of honey
will catch more flies than a Gallon of Vinegar.

Thou canst not joke an Enemy into a Friend;
but thou may'st a Friend into an Enemy.

Tis better leave for an enemy at one's death, than
beg of a friend in one's life.

When befriended, remember it:
When you befriend, forget it.

Promises may get thee Friends, but Nonperformance
will turn them into Enemies.

The rotten Apple spoils his Companion.

He makes a Foe who makes a jest.

If you wou'd be reveng'd of your enemy, govern yourself.

'Tis great Confidence in a Friend to tell him *your* Faults, greater to tell him *his*.

Some *Worth* it argues, a Friend's *Worth* to know; *Virtue* to own the Virtue of a Foe.

Hear no ill of a Friend, nor speak any of an Enemy.

Anoint a villain and he'll stab you, stab him & he'l anoint you.

Who judges best of a Man, his Enemies or himself?

Now I've a sheep and a cow, every body bids me good morrow.

The same man cannot be both Friend and Flatterer.

Beware of meat twice boil'd, & an old foe reconcil'd.

Knaves & Nettles are akin; stroak 'em kindly,
yet they'll sting.

Friendship cannot live with *Ceremony,* nor without
Civility.

If any man flatters me, I'll flatter him again;
tho' he were my best Friend.

Lend Money to an Enemy, and thou'lt gain him,
to a Friend and thou'lt lose him.

Do good to thy Friend to keep him,
to thy enemy to gain him.

There is no little enemy.

An open Foe may prove a curse;
But a pretended friend is worse.

Wouldst thou confound thine Enemy, be good thy self.

A true Friend is the best Possession.

No better relation than a prudent & faithful Friend.

A false Friend and a Shadow,
attend only while the Sun shines.

A Father's a Treasure; a Brother's a Comfort;
a Friend is both.

Be slow in chusing a Friend, slower in changing.

VICE
&
VIRTUE

No longer virtuous no longer free, is a Maxim as true with regard to a private Person as a Common-wealth.

Learning to the Studious; Riches to the Careful; Power to the Bold; Heaven to the Virtuous.

Seek Virtue, and, of that possest,
To Providence, resign the rest.

The excellency of hogs is fatness, of men virtue.

Hast thou virtue? acquire also the graces & beauties of virtue.

You may be more happy than Princes,
if you will be more virtuous.

Against Diseases here, the strongest Fence,
Is the defensive Virtue, Abstinence

Virtue and Happiness are Mother and Daughter.

He is ill cloth'd, who is bare of Virtue.

Virtue and a Trade, are a Child's best Portion.

Relation without friendship, friendship without power, power without will, will without effect, effect without profit, & profit without vertue, are not worth a farto.

When ☿ and ♂ in ♂ lie,
Then, Maids, whate'er is ask'd of you, deny.

Prosperity discovers Vice, Adversity Virtue.

Search others for their virtues, thy self for thy vices.

Avoid dishonest Gain: No price
Can recompence the Pangs of Vice.

Tho' Modesty is a Virtue, Bashfulness is a Vice.

'Tis easier to suppress the first Desire,
than to satisfy all that follow it.

The second Vice is Lying; the first is Running in Debt.

Keep flax from fire, youth from gaming.

Sell not virtue to purchase wealth, nor Liberty
to purchase power.

What maintains one Vice would bring up two Children.

Caesar did not merit the triumphal Car,
more than he that conquers himself.

The Honey is sweet, but the Bee has a Sting.

How few there are who have courage enough to own
their Faults, or resolution enough to mend them!

A Plowman on his Legs is higher than a Gentleman
on his Knees.

Pain wastes the Body, Pleasures the Understanding.

Be at War with your Vices, at Peace with your Neighbours, and let every New-Year find you a better Man.

A Man without ceremony has need of great merit in its place.

With the old Almanack and the old Year,
Leave thy old Vices, tho' ever so dear.

What more valuable than Gold? Diamonds. Than Diamonds? Virtue.

Virtue may not always make a Face handsome, but *Vice* will certainly make it ugly.

Honour thy Father and Mother, *i.e.* Live so as to be an Honour to them tho' they are dead.

He is a Governor that governs his Passions, and he a Servant that serves them.

A Cypher and Humility make the other Figures & Virtues of ten-fold Value.

Mankind are very odd Creatures: One Half censure what they practise, the other half practise what they censure; the rest always say and do as they ought.

Vice knows she's ugly, so puts on her Mask.

Beatus esse sine Virtute, nemo potest.

There is much difference between imitating a good man, and counterfeiting him.

Many a Man thinks he is buying Pleasure, when he is really selling himself a Slave to it.

Glass, China, and Reputation, are easily crack'd, and never well mended.

To be humble to Superiors is Duty, to Equals Courtesy, to Inferiors Nobleness.

Don't value a man for the Quality he is of, but for the Qualities he possesses.

An ill Wound, but not an ill Name, may be healed.

The Devil sweetens Poison with Honey.

'Tis a Shame that your Family is an Honour to you!
You ought to be an Honour to your Family.

> Sustain'd by Reason still, unmov'd he stood,
> And steady bore against th' opposing Flood.
> He durst correct what Nature form'd amiss,
> And forc'd unwilling Virtue to be his.

Much Virtue in Herbs, little in Men.

Who is strong? He that can conquer his bad Habits

Retirement does not always secure Virtue;
Lot was upright in the City, wicked in the Mountain.

Innocence is its own Defence.

'Tis easier to prevent bad habits than to break them.

Act uprightly, and despise Calumny; Dirt may stick to
a Mud Wall, but not to polish'd Marble.

The noblest question in the world is,
What Good may I do in it?

None but the well bred man knows how to confess a
fault, or acknowledge himself in an error.

Avoid dishonest Gain: No price
Can recompence the Pangs of Vice.

A great talker may be no Fool,
but he is one that relies on him.

WISDOM
&
FOOLISHNESS

You may sometimes be much in the wrong,
in owning your being in the right.

There are no fools so troublesome as those that have wit.

Two Faults of one a Fool will make;
He half repairs, that owns & does forsake.

Wise Men learn by others harms; Fools by their own.

Most Fools think they are only ignorant.

Liberality is not giving much but giving wisely.

The Brave and the Wise can both pity and excuse;
when Cowards and Fools shew no Mercy.

The Family of Fools is ancient.

A great Talker may be no Fool,
but he is one that relies on him.

He's a Fool that cannot conceal his Wisdom.

Fools make feasts and wise men eat them.

The most exquisite Folly is made of Wisdom spun too
fine.

The learned Fool writes his Nonsense in better Language
than the unlearned; but still 'tis Nonsense.

He that lives well, is learned enough.

Admiration is the Daughter of Ignorance.

It is Ill-Manners to silence a Fool, and Cruelty
to let him go on.

Hear *Reason,* or she'll make you feel her.

Blame-all and *Praise-all* are two blockheads.

Some men grow mad by studying much to know,
But who grows mad by studying good to grow.

A learned blockhead is a greater blockhead
than an ignorant one.

You will be careful, if you are wise;
How you touch Men's Religion, or Credit, or Eyes.

Sound, & sound Doctrine, may pass through a Ram's
Horn, and a Preacher, without straitening the one, or
amending the other.

As Charms are nonsense, Nonsense is a Charm.

An ounce of wit that is bought,
Is worth a pound that is taught.

The heart of a fool is in his mouth, but the mouth
of a wise man is in his heart.

He that has neither fools, whores nor beggars among his kindred, is the son of a thunder gust.

Where Sense is wanting, every thing is wanting.

A Man of Knowledge like a rich Soil, feeds
If not a world of Corn, a world of Weeds.

Some are weatherwise, some are otherwise.

To be intimate with a foolish Friend,
is like going to bed to a Razor.

The fool hath made a vow, I guess,
Never to let the Fire have peace.

When Reason preaches, if you won't hear her she'll box your Ears.

Proud Modern Learning despises the antient:
School-men are now laught at by *School-boys*.

Fools need Advice most, but wise Men only are the better for it.

Can grave and formal pass for wise,
When Men the solemn Owl despise?

Being ignorant is not so much a Shame,
as being unwilling to learn.

Of learned Fools I have seen ten times ten,
Of unlearned wise men I have seen a hundred.

Experience keeps a dear school, yet Fools will learn
in no other.

Reading makes a full Man, Meditation a profound Man,
discourse a clear Man.

Force shites upon Reason's Back.

He has chang'd his one ey'd horse for a blind one.

What signifies knowing the Names,
if you know not the Natures of Things.

Ever since Follies have pleas'd, Fools have been able to
divert.

A fine genius in his own country, is like gold in the mine.

Here comes the Orator! with his Flood of Words,
and his Drop of Reason.

Interest which blinds some People, enlightens others.

Learn of the skilful: He that teaches himself,
hath a fool for his master.

Want of Care does us more Damage than
Want of Knowledge.

Fools multiply folly.

Genius without Education is like Silver in the Mine.

Men differ daily, about things which are subject to
Sense, is it likely then they should agree about things
invisible.

Life with Fools consists in Drinking;
With the wise Man, Living's Thinking.

A Mob's a Monster; Heads enough, but no Brains.

At 20 years of age the Will reigns; at 30 the Wit; at 40 the Judgment.

Be neither silly, nor cunning, but wise.

Sampson with his *strong Body,* had a *weak Head,* or he would not have laid it in a Harlot's Lap.

Most of the Learning in use, is of no great Use.

Tricks and Trechery are the Practice of Fools, that have not Wit enough to be honest.

A Mob's a Monster; Heads enough, but no Brains.

The Doors of Wisdom are never shut.

Good Sense is a Thing all need, few have, and none think they want.

Would you persuade, speak of Interest, not of Reason.

If what most men admire, they would despise,
'Twould look as if mankind were growing wise.

The Things which hurt, instruct.

After crosses and losses men grow humbler & wiser.

Tim was so learned, that he could name a Horse in
nine Languages: So ignorant, that he bought a Cow
to ride on.

He that knows nothing of it, may by chance be a
Prophet; while the wisest that is may happen to miss.

The Wise and Brave dares own that he was wrong.

The old Man has given all to his Son: O fool!
to undress thy self before thou art going to bed.

The first Degree of Folly, is to conceit one's self wise;
the second to profess it; the third to despise Counsel.

The wise Man draws more Advantage from his Enemies,
than the Fool from his Friends.

A wise Man will desire no more, than what he may get justly, use soberly, distribute chearfully, and leave contentedly.

Many complain of their Memory, few of their Judgment.

Half Wits talk much but say little.

Doors and walls are fools paper.

If your head is wax, don't walk in the Sun.

Who knows a fool, must know his brother;
For one will recommend another.

There's many witty men whose brains can't fill their bellies.

SLOTH
&
DILIGENCE

Jack *Little* sow'd little, & little he'll reap.

'Tis a laudable Ambition, that aims at being better than his Neighbours.

Little Strokes,
Fell great Oaks.

God helps them that help themselves.

The Master piece of Man, is to live to the purpose.

At the working man's house hunger looks in but dares not enter.

'Tis easy to frame a good bold resolution;
But hard is the Task that concerns execution.

The Master's Eye will do more Work than both his
Hands.

The sleeping Fox catches no poultry. Up! up!

God gives all Things to Industry.

Sloth and Silence are a Fool's Virtues.

Great Talkers, little Doers.

By diligence and patience, the mouse bit in two the
cable.

O Lazy-Bones! Dost thou think God would have given
thee Arms and Legs, if he had not design'd thou
should'st use them.

Up, Sluggard, and waste not life;
in the grave will be sleeping enough.

Trouble springs from *Idleness*; *Toil* from *Ease*.

Strive to be the *greatest* Man in your Country, and you may be disappointed; Strive to be the *best,* and you may succeed: He may well win the race that runs by himself.

The Cat in Gloves catches no Mice.

Well done, is twice done.

The favour of the Great is no inheritance.

Diligence overcomes Difficulties, Sloth makes them.

Sloth (like Rust) consumes faster than Labour wears: the used Key is always bright.

Adieu, my Task's ended.

No Wood without Bark.

He that by the Plow would thrive,
himself must either hold or drive.

The Day is short, the Work great, the Workmen lazy, the Wages high, the Master urgeth; Up, then, and be doing.

Saying and *Doing* have quarrel'd and parted.

Well done is better than well said.

Help, Hands; For I have no Lands.

Laziness travels so slowly, that *Poverty* soon overtakes him.

A life of leisure, and a life of laziness, are two things.

Speak little, do much.

All things are easy to Industry,
All things difficult to *Sloth*.

Plough deep, while Sluggards sleep;
And you shall have Corn, to sell and to keep.

The idle Man is the Devil's Hireling; whose Livery is Rags, whose Diet and Wages are Famine and Diseases.

If you wou'd not be forgotten
As soon as you are dead and rotten,
Either write things worth reading,
or do things worth the writing.

Industry need not wish.

No man e'er was glorious, who was not laborious.

There are lazy Minds as well as lazy Bodies.

Diligence is the Mother of Good-Luck.

Be always asham'd to catch thy self idle.

The diligent Spinner has a large Shift.

He that lives upon Hope, dies farting.

What's proper, is becoming: See the Blacksmith with his white Silk Apron!

The good Spinner hath a large Shift.

He that would catch Fish, must venture his Bait.

LOVE
&
BENEVOLENCE

A good Example is the best sermon.

If thou dost ill, the joy fades, not the pains;
If well, the pain doth fade, the joy remains.

Great-Almsgiving, lessens no Man's Living.

To bear other Peoples Afflictions, every one
has Courage enough, and to spare.

The Sun never repents of the good he does,
nor does he ever demand a recompence.

A long Life may not be good enough,
but a good Life is long enough.

Ill Company is like a dog who dirts those most, that he loves best.

Proportion your Charity to the Strength of your Estate, or God will proportion your Estate to the Weakness of your Charity.

Each year one vicious habit rooted out,
In time might make the worst Man good throughout.

You may drive a gift without a gimblet.

Love, and be *loved.*

Love your Enemies, for they tell you your Faults.

Nothing so popular as GOODNESS.

There was never a good Knife made of bad Steel.

Who pleasure gives,
Shall joy receive.

Good-Will, like the Wind, floweth where it listeth.

Gifts burst rocks.

A good Man is seldom uneasy, an ill one never easie.

Graft good Fruit all, or graft not at all.

Great souls with gen'rous pity melt;
Which coward tyrants never felt.

Love well, whip well.

Setting too good an Example is a Kind of Slander
seldom forgiven; 'tis *Scandalum Magnatum*.

'Tis a strange Forest that has no rotten Wood in't
And a strange Kindred that all are good in't.

To God we owe fear and love; to our neighbours justice
and charity; to our selves prudence and sobriety.

Doing an Injury puts you below your Enemy;
Revenging one makes you but *even* with him; *Forgiving*
it sets you *above* him.

Love, Cough, & a Smoke, can't well be hid.

If you'd be belov'd, make yourself amiable.

Don't overload Gratitude; if you do, she'll kick.

If thou would'st live long, live well;
for Folly and Wickedness shorten Life.

If you would be loved, love and be loveable.

Love thy Neighbour; yet don't pull down your Hedge.

There are no ugly Loves, nor handsome Prisons.

Most People return small Favours, acknowledge
middling ones, and repay great ones with Ingratitude.

What's given shines,
What's receiv'd is rusty.

All Mankind are beholden to him that is kind to the Good.

Great Beauty, great strength, & great Riches, are really & truly of no great Use; a right Heart exceeds all.

Love and *Tooth-ach* have many Cures, but none infallible, except *Possession* and *Dispossession*.

Half-Hospitality opens his Doors and shuts up his Countenance.

If you would reap Praise you must sow the Seeds, Gentle Words and useful Deeds.

When you're good to others, you are best to yourself.

When befriended, remember it: When you befriend, forget it.

Fear to do ill, and you need fear nought else.

As often as we do good, we sacrifice.

Who dainties love, shall Beggars prove.

Let our Fathers and Grandfathers be valued for *their* Goodness, ourselves for our own.

There is no Man so bad, but he secretly respects the Good.

Love & lordship hate companions.

CUNNING
&
WIT

Pretty & Witty, will wound if they hit ye.

The Wolf sheds his Coat once a Year, his Disposition never.

There are no fools so troublesome as those that have wit.

You may be too cunning for One, but not for All.

Ben beats his Pate, and fancy wit will come;
But he may knock, there's no body at home.

Strange! that a Man who has wit enough to write a Satyr; should have folly enough to publish it.

Cunning proceeds from Want of Capacity.

One Man may be more cunning than another,
but not more cunning than every body else.

Words may shew a man's Wit, but *Actions* his Meaning.

Many Foxes grow grey, but few grow good.

Many would live by their Wits, but break for want of
Stock.

Better slip with foot than tongue.

Cold & cunning come from the north:
but cunning sans wisdom is nothing worth.

Don't think so much of your own Cunning, as to forget
other Mens: A cunning Man is overmatch'd by a
cunning Man and a Half.

The cunning man steals a horse, the wise man lets him.